AMANDA GORMAN

by Jehan Jones-Radgowski

PEBBLE
a capstone imprint

Published by Pebble, an imprint of Capstone
1710 Roe Crest Drive, North Mankato, Minnesota 56003
capstonepub.com

Library of Congress Cataloging-in-Publication Data
Names: Jones-Radgowski, Jehan, author.
Title: Amanda Gorman / by Jehan Jones-Radgowski.
Description: North Mankato, Minnesota : Pebble, [2023] | Series: Biographies | Includes bibliographical references and index. | Audience: Ages 5-8. | Audience: Grades K-1. | Summary: "How much do you know about Amanda Gorman? Find out the facts you need to know about this impressive young poet. You'll learn about the childhood, challenges, and accomplishments of this rising star"— Provided by publisher.
Identifiers: LCCN 2021061404 (print) | LCCN 2021061405 (ebook) | ISBN 9781666350524 (hardcover) | ISBN 9781666350753 (paperback) | ISBN 9781666350715 (pdf) | ISBN 9781666350630 (kindle edition)
Subjects: LCSH: Gorman, Amanda, 1998—-Juvenile literature. | African American women poets—Biography—Juvenile literature. | Poets, American—21st century—Biography—Juvenile literature.
Classification: LCC PS3607.O59774 Z69 2023 (print) | LCC PS3607.O59774 (ebook) | DDC 811/.6 [B]—dc23/eng/20220111
LC record available at https://lccn.loc.gov/2021061404
LC ebook record available at https://lccn.loc.gov/2021061405

Editorial Credits
Editor: Mandy Robbins; Designer: Hilary Wacholz; Media Researchers: Jo Miller and Pam Mitsakos; Production Specialist: Tori Abraham

Image Credits
Alamy: Alto Vintage Images, 19, dpa picture alliance, 5, 17, Patti McConville, 23, WENN Rights Ltd, 13; Associated Press: zz/John Nacion/STAR MAX/IPx, Cover, 1; Getty Images: 6381380, 25, Jared Siskin, 29, John Chapple, 9, kali9, 21, Leif Skoogfors, 12, Paul Marotta, 15, VALERIE MACON, 26; Shutterstock: divanov, 10, logoboom, 11, Marc Venema, 24, Strike First, 7

All internet sites appearing in back matter were available and accurate when this book was sent to press.

Table of Contents

Words in **bold** are in the glossary.

Who Is Amanda Gorman?

On January 20, 2021, Amanda Gorman made history. President Joe Biden was being sworn in. At the ceremony, Amanda read her poem. She was the youngest **poet** to ever do so. The poem was called "The Hill We Climb."

On that day, other people wore gray, black, or blue. Amanda stood out. She wore a bold yellow coat and a red headband.

Amanda spoke of America. An America full of promise. She said we are climbing a great hill. She called on Americans to do better.

Growing Up In Two Worlds

Amanda was born on March 7, 1998. She grew up in Los Angeles, California. Amanda has a twin sister named Gabrielle. She also has an older brother named Spencer. The family lived in a two-bedroom apartment.

Amanda was raised by her mother, Joan Wicks. Joan was a single mother. She was an English teacher. Joan helped Amanda learn to love books.

Los Angeles, California

Joan sent Amanda to private school. It was a 25-minute drive to school each day. Amanda passed many neighborhoods on her way to school. She saw how people lived differently.

Amanda went to New Roads School. This school taught art. It also focused on helping people. This school was very **diverse**. There were children from many backgrounds. Some were rich and others were poor.

New Roads School

A home in a wealthy area in California

Amanda felt like she lived in two different worlds. The houses near her school were big. They had large yards. Amanda lived in a small apartment. She also felt different from other kids. She would rather read books than play on the playground.

Amanda's mom didn't let her watch much TV. Amanda didn't mind. She was very creative. She made up her own plays and wrote songs.

An apartment in a poor California neighborhood

Heroes and Challenges

Many people have **inspired** Amanda. One is the poet Maya Angelou. She was the first Black poet and the first woman to read at a U.S. president's swearing-in ceremony. Her poem was called "On the Pulse of Morning."

Maya Angelou

Toni Morrison

Amanda also liked Toni Morrison. She loved Morrison's book *The Bluest Eye*. The girl on the cover was Black like Amanda. She had never seen a cover like that before. Amanda wanted every child to see someone like them on a cover.

Activist Malala Yousafzai also inspired Amanda. Amanda heard her speak about the rights of girls to go to school.

Amanda wants to create change. She doesn't care what a person's skin color is. She doesn't care about **gender** or religion. She doesn't care if someone is attracted to men or women. And she doesn't care how much money a person makes. Amanda wants everyone to be treated fairly.

Malala Yousafzai

Amanda has faced many challenges. One is speaking. Amanda does not hear the same as others. Because of this, she struggles to say the letter R. A word like "rainbow" is hard for Amanda to say. Amanda tried to avoid "R" words. She would say "young woman" instead of "girl."

Amanda's poem "The Hill We Climb" has a lot of "R" words. Amanda practiced reading her poem many times.

Amanda Writes

Amanda wrote songs as a young child. She wrote her first poem in the third grade. It was about being alone. Writing poems made Amanda feel better.

Amanda had a teacher named Shelly Fredman. She wanted to help Amanda write more. She gave her sandwiches when Amanda wrote a poem. Amanda loved the sandwiches.

19

Writing helps Amanda say how she feels. It makes her feel powerful. She wanted other kids to have that feeling.

In 2016, she created One Pen One Page. With this group, Amanda helped students write. She taught them poetry. She helped them share their ideas. She helped them write about their feelings. It made them feel powerful too.

Amanda kept writing poems. In 2015, she put out a book of poetry. She was 17 years old. Her book was called *The One for Whom Food Is Not Enough*. In 2017, Amanda was named the best young poet in America.

In 2021, Amanda put out three more books. One is for children. It is called *Change Sings: A Children's Anthem*. Amanda wants her writing to make children feel powerful. Her other two books are also poetry. They focus on hope.

"FOR THERE IS
ALWAYS LIGHT,
IF ONLY WE'RE
BRAVE ENOUGH
TO SEE IT.
IF ONLY WE'RE
BRAVE ENOUGH
TO BE IT."
–Amanda Gorman

Amanda has read her poetry in many places. She read at the Empire State Building in 2019. It is in New York City. It is one of the tallest buildings in the world.

Empire State Building

2021 Super Bowl at Raymond
James Stadium in Tampa, Florida

In 2021, Amanda became the
first poet to read at the Super
Bowl. The Super Bowl is a big
football game. Many people think
professional athletes are heroes.
But at the game, Amanda read her
poem about everyday heroes.

Future Plans

Amanda went to college at Harvard University. It is the oldest college in America. Harvard gave Amanda a **scholarship**. She finished school there in 2020.

What is next for Amanda? She is already a poet. She is an author. Amanda is an activist.

Amanda wants to be the president of the United States. She first stated this in the 6th grade. U.S. law says a person must be 35 years old to be president. Amanda will have to wait.

We don't know what Amanda will do in the future. But we do know she will help make the world a better place.

Important Dates

1998	Amanda is born.
2015	Amanda **publishes** her book of poetry.
2016	Amanda starts One Pen One Page.
2017	Amanda is named a National Youth Poet Laureate. A laureate is an important poet.
2020	Amanda graduates from Harvard.
2021	Amanda speaks at Joe Biden's swearing-in ceremony, called an inauguration.
2021	Amanda reads her poetry at the Super Bowl.

Fast Facts

Name:
Amanda Gorman

Roles:
poet, author, activist

Life dates:
Born March 7, 1998

Key accomplishments:
Amanda is the first National Youth Poet Laureate. She was the youngest speaker at a presidential inauguration. She is also a best-selling author and a Harvard graduate.

Glossary

activist (AK-tuh-vist)—a person who works for social or political change

diverse (dye-VURSS)—when people come from a variety of backgrounds

gender (JEHN-dur)—the expression of male or female-ness

inspire (in-SPIRE)—to influence or encourage someone in a good way to do something

poet (PO-eht)—a person whose writing is arranged in lines that have a rhythm or beat and sometimes rhyme

publish (PUB-lish)—to produce and distribute a book

scholarship (SKOL-ur-ship)—money given to a student to pay for school

Read More

Briscoe, Eyrn. *Amanda Gorman*. Ann Arbor, MI: Cherry Lake Publishing, 2022.

Maslo, Lina. *Free As a Bird: the Story of Malala*. New York: Balzer + Bray, An Imprint of HarperCollins Publishers, 2018.

Vegara, Maria Isabel Sánchez. *Amanda Gorman*. London, UK: Frances Lincoln Children's Books, 2022.

Internet Sites

The Children's Poetry Archive
childrens.poetryarchive.org

Poems for Kids
poets.org/poems-kids

Poetry for Children Written by Black Authors
nypl.org/blog/2021/02/17/childrens-poetry-black-authors

Index

About the Author

Jehan Jones-Radgowski is the author of seven children's books. She received a bachelor's degree from George Mason University and her M.A. from George Washington University. She is also a U.S. Foreign Service Officer. She has lived with her three kids, husband, and dog worldwide, including the Dominican Republic, Germany, South Africa, Spain, the Russian Federation, the United States, and Venezuela.